Game Design Philosophy

As you read this book, you will come to learn that the philosophies behind Game Design and the *Game Design Guidelines* also work in most situations you will encounter throughout life, and just like with life, it's important to have and understand purpose.   Therefore, in order to understand the guidelines for Game Design, we must first define Game Design.

-What is Game Design?

So what is Game Design?   It's the entire process from concept creation to contents creation, release and often including post-release management and administration of any form of interactive entertainment.   Since the majority of my professional experience in Game Design has been on next generation consoles, the focus will be put on console games.   But the guidelines we will go over in this book can also be used when designing anything and everything from board games or casino style card games to

5 minutes mobile games and high-end PC games.

-What does a Game Designer do?

This is another issue we have to define before going over the guidelines because simply hearing that someone designs interactive entertainment doesn't really say a lot to the average person, or even sometimes doesn't really hold solid ground even in the gaming industry.

When I was on my first multi-million seller AAA title, the Lead Game Designer on that project would often say that a Game Designer does everything the other staff members (Programmers and Graphic Designs, etc.) do not do.   In my experience, a Game Designer will do everything the other staff members do not do as well as many things they do.   I will go over this subject in much more detail during the guidelines.

-Who can become a Game Designer?

I assume that the majority of you, who are reading this book are either already in or considering entering the game industry and most likely have an interest in the field of Game Design, and to give you hope, I would like to be able to say "anyone," but this isn't always the case.   Like with most fields of creation and many outside of creation, there are restrictions and limitations that might keep some people from becoming a Game Designer.

In my case, I had 5 years of University, getting 2 degrees studying both natural language and computer language, including Game Programming, as well as I had an internship at a mid-sized company for several months as a Game Programmer before I got into a large company as a Game Designer.   Do you really need all this?   No.   I have met people in the industry who have great positions who are high school dropouts, as well as people who have studied at some of the most prestigious Universities in the entire world.   I have met great Game Designers and in my opinion poor Game Designers on both ends.   The only thing you really do need to become a great Game

Designer is PIFA (Persistence, Intellect, Flexibility, and Acceptance).   During the guidelines we will indulge ourselves with the exact meaning and reasons for these qualities.

   Now, without further ado let's take a look at philosophies or guidelines that all great Game Designers should keep in the back of their minds…

Game Design Guidelines

Table of Contents:

1. Understand the Concept of Every Aspect of the Project

Every item, every sound, every texture, every wall; invisible or otherwise has a purpose, and every project has *concepts*. Every aspect of the project must not contradict the overall concept of the project itself and all other concepts above that of said aspect.

Before we go further, we must make it clear what a concept is. Simply put, it is a goal, an objective, a purpose, a reason. Even more simply put it is *what you want to do*, not to be confused with how it is done. This also very easily applies to real life. An example would be if you see a person riding the train and wonder what this person's current objective is, because riding the train would simply be a means to the actual concept of the venture. This person may be heading out to a super market to purchase certain ingredients to cook a nice meal to entertain a date on an anniversary. The main concept of his or her entire venture would be to have an enjoyable anniversary dinner, and the train, purchasing of ingredients, cooking of the food, etc. would all be means to achieve this goal. During such a venture there could also be sub-concepts in play. Why did he or she choose that train car? Perhaps the goal of that action was to relax in a relatively empty train car, or the train was leaving and he or she had to board the train before the doors closed, or perhaps it's the closest train car to the exit he or she wants to be at when exiting the train. Whatever the reasoning behind this person's actions, there is most certainly some kind of concept, and in Game Design it is extremely crucial to understand this point.

Let's give a more game-themed example of why sub-concepts are also important to understand. If you're on a project and the highest concept of the project is "*horror*," then the concept of every aspect of the game should have no direct conflict with horror unless it serves the ultimate goal of enhancing the horror experience itself. Now, with a single concept ruling over one project, things can get confusing. Sub-concepts are set in place to help further define the main concept and how other things relate to this concept.   Our example of horror could actually mean a large number of things. Aliens in space, ghosts in the forest, zombies in a city, being completely isolated from all other life – all of these things could easily be considered horror, yet it might be difficult to create a game about being completely alone in the forest city in space with the ghosts of zombie aliens.   Therefore, before a project comes into full production, several deciding factors must be determined ahead of time to clarify the concept and various sub-concepts of a project.   Sharing these concepts with a team or learning these concepts from the concept creators is vital to being an active and useful member of any project.

Points to keep in mind when…

Creating a Concept: If you are the concept creator you need to keep a few things in mind. First, keep your concept simple and easy to understand.   One of the most famous concepts for one of the most famous video games is simply one word, "Jump."   We will refer to this concept as an example in other guidelines as well.

   Understanding a Concept: If anyone but yourself is creating concepts on a project, especially if it is the overall concept, you must have a grasp on that concept.   If you are worried you may not understand what the concept of something on a project is, be sure to ask.

   Following a Concept: Once a concept has been made, you need to train yourself into it becoming second nature to you for the duration of work to which that concept applies.   Until it becomes second nature, always second guess your decisions and reference the concepts that exist to make sure your ideas or work fit the concept.   Voice your thoughts and try to explain in words how your idea or content relates to the overall concept of the project, and how that will make the game more entertaining in the end.

Exercise on Concepts: Write down the name of your favorite existing game and beside it write as many answers as you can think of for what the main concept of that game could possibly be.

2. See the Essence (≒concept) of All Actions and Statements

Without a doubt more than one person reading this book likely read parts of the previous guideline with some doubts in mind.   Perhaps the "person riding the train" in the concept explanation is a certain character who simply loves trains and his entire purpose for being on the train is actually to enjoy the train ride.   Sure, that may be a possibility, but the point of that whole statement in the previous outline was not to talk about trains, but to make a point regarding the importance of understanding concepts.

Therefore, always try to view the *essence* of each subject.   Like with any rule anywhere, these are not rules set in stone and there are exceptions and perhaps even existing examples of situations that don't fit these rules.   However, viewing the essence of a subject means understanding the true meaning behind a statement.   Even the most ludicrous and sometimes extremely rude statements often have hidden essences to them.

A prime example of when most people don't understand the essence of a situation would be when you are a child, you would usually be frightened by an angry parent or teacher, but their true intentions are for your education or well-being.   Now, if you read this statement thinking to yourself "but my situation…" the entire time, then you're in luck because we have another prime example of missing the essence of a statement.   If you look hard enough you can find situational excuses or even existing examples that go against any other action or statement, but if it isn't in correlation with the actual intent of said action or statement, then the point is lost for both the sending and receiving parties.

This is a problem I personally found a hard time to get over, always trying to be "smarter" than everyone else, even if that means always trying to find exceptions to rules.   When I was first being trained as a Game Designer, I had a master-apprentice relationship for 2 years with an industry veteran Director, and one of the first things he ever said to me was "You are always

100% wrong." Of course, I wasn't too happy hearing that from a guy I had just met at the time, and to me it just seemed plain mean. It wasn't actually until much, much later until I finally realized the essence of his statement, and it's a great life lesson and a fantastic mind set to have when dealing with other human beings.

So, I will reword it to make it slightly more direct, and pass this life lesson onto you. *Every time anyone ever disagrees with you from now on, you are wrong.*

Points to keep in mind with…

Understanding an Essence: There are often cases where people unintentionally try to make their points in very abstract ways. A few points in this book may also be abstract. If you are in the situation where you can clarify with a person, never be afraid to ask; especially if it has an effect on the quality of your work.

Exercise on Essences:　Consider the possible meanings of the statement I made above, "*Every time anyone ever disagrees with you from now on, you are wrong.*"　Considering I wrote this in the section about seeing the essence of actions and statements, I think it might be obvious that there is another meaning behind that statement.　You may find the correct answer to this later in this book.

3. Know your Target Audience

A target audience is important in most industries, but is usually thought of as simply a way of marketing.   Whether or not a target audience is made public, you will find that many adults will have no shame playing fun games set in cartoony worlds with abstract characters, and you will also find many young kids playing very photo-real and violent war games, obviously with their parents' consent.   If this is the case, why bother to set a target at all?

Reasons for deciding this vary, including the obvious market research or even certain contract bindings.   However, even if you had no legal limitations and didn't care too much about trying to optimize sales, it is still best to have a set and specific target audience.   Having a target audience in no way means you are actually limiting potential users, since when making a game, especially with a team there will be disagreements over issues that are often nothing more than preference of a team member. However, if there is a target audience set during the initial stages of the game, these arguments and perplexes can be avoided by siding with for what statistics would say that target would show the most interest. On a large project usually a project lead or initial design document creator will have decided on a target, so make sure you know who this target is when designing game elements.

There are also times during projects when a target, usually for marketing purposes is put even above a concept. I've been on projects where we had to ensure that the content rating was aimed at people of a certain age group, and to do so we had to add certain mature content and take some away, because there are also many people in the world who take the rating of a game personally and won't purchase a game with content rated above or below their age ranges. It is also important to note that some countries rate games more strictly based on certain content. Germany and Japan for example, are far sterner with violence in games, while America and several European countries are sometimes strict with sexual content. Despite certain instances where having a target audience may possibly hinder creativity, once more I'd like to repeat myself and say the main purpose of having a target audience is to *keep the flow of creativity smooth*.

Also remember that your target audience is not always the project's target audience. If you are handing in a document within the project team alone, your target audience is whomever will be reading said document; most likely your boss or the project leaders.

Things to keep in mind when…

Deciding a target: If you are the one who decides a target audience there are a few things to think about before deciding. Does your target audience fit with your project's concept? Is it easy to define this target audience? What problems could having said target audience possibly cause?

Knowing your target audience: Make sure you spend at least some time learning who and what your target audience is and what their likes and dislikes may be.   At times it may feel like unnecessary behavior analysis, but it is a good way to determine which idea to pick when multiple ideas fit the overall concept.   Many of the same rules apply when the target audience for a specific task is different from the overall target audience.   For example, if your boss hates reading, you want to avoid unnecessary text in documents you present to him or her.

Your project has no determined target audience: Make one, or have someone with that authority do so.   Although not as important as a concept, many times a project's final decisions will come down to who the target audience is.   If you have full authority on a project and wish to rule with an iron fist, then to make things easy for yourself, *you* can be the main target audience.   In this case, if it meets the concept, whatever you like is whatever works.

4. Level Design through Psychological Control

A good Game Designer will generally be able to control the majority of the people who play his or her game.   This is a necessary skill in most Game Designer positions, but a must for Level Designers.   Whether linear or open world and free running, controlling the user is something most major games will have.

In linear games or linear areas of certain games, this is often done by force, giving the player only one option of progression, whereas more open games or areas with multiple paths will often use more psychological methods to lead the player to or from a specific area. Some easy examples would be radars, maps, mission objectives and other UI indicating the player's next objective.   Other examples which might not seem as obvious to players would include dirt paths through grassy hills and a trail through a forest, a line of collectable items like coins which may benefit the player in other ways, or simply well placed landmarks which visually spark the interest of the player.   All of these are examples of some of the many ways Game Designers will use to ensure that the majority of people who play their games will follow certain paths or visit certain areas.   Even if the player can go back at any moment in the game, the psychological aspects used, such as visuals and narratives will keep the player wanting to move forward.

For a Level Designer this means it's not just about putting together a level, but rather knowing exactly what the player is thinking at every instance during the course of the level.   Using elements in the game, the Level Designer will essentially be able to take control of the player's thoughts and actions while still allowing the player to maintain the illusion of total and complete free will.

Of course, depending on time constraints or technological and financial limitations, or in some cases simply a lack of creativity; the extreme linear option is often chosen.   However, despite the word linear often being viewed as bad in modern day games, if it properly fits the concept and amplifies the fun of the game itself, a completely linear game or area of a game may be the best choice with or without possible limitations.

It's easy to look at multiplayer shooter games and determine whether or not these games have well put together levels depending on the game mode, the size of the levels and the placement of items and gimmicks in each level.   In most multiplayer shooting games, the objective of the Game Designer is to get the participants to end up in the same general area so a battle can take place.   This can be done by placing the mission objective such as a flag to capture or base to take over in a certain area, or simply by placing some of the best weapons in the game that each player wants in certain areas.   These sorts of tactics draw players towards certain areas to keep the game entertaining.   If you find yourself playing a lot of multiplayer shooting games where you almost never run into other players, there is a high chance the levels were not properly designed for multiplayer.

Things to keep in mind when…

Creating a new Level or Area: Assuming you already have the concept in mind, one other thing to remember is the System Design of a game, and the abilities of a player.   Is a player is able to fly freely through any stage or is a player limited to basic running and walking? Can the player jump or roll?   Does the player lock onto enemies automatically?   Without having a firm grasp on all of these aspects, it is extremely difficult to create a level which allows the creator to control the player's actions.

Balancing a Level or Area: Getting into the mind of the player often means getting out of your own mind.   If you are on a team, have other members of the team play your level or area and watch exactly how they play, what direction their player or camera face, what they look at first.   If the majority does not match your intentions you should study the reasons behind this.   It could be something as simple as the lighting in a stage.

Adding hidden sections to an Area: Hidden items or sections in a level are often fun and add value to a game.   However, in most cases you want the player to find these elements, otherwise there really would be nearly no point in putting them in the game in the first place.   That means often placing them slightly within visual range of where the players are most likely to look, or showing the players what they have missed after the fact as to encourage them to return to those areas later.   A simple collection screen menu can be a viable solution, or perhaps something such as showing the player a hidden item on the other side of a door the second a door closes which can no longer be opened.   The placement of hidden items in levels is probably one of the most creatively challenging tasks within Level Design.

5. Understanding and Using Meaningful Decisions

Meaningful decisions here will be defined as the *reasons for an option of choice* during a game.   This sounds extremely confusing, so let's try to describe this in a more simplistic way. This is very closely related to controlling the player's actions.   A game with deep meaningful decisions consists of constant situations where a player will be given a choice as well as incentive towards all available choices.   A simple example would be having an item or two on one path which also has enemies lurking around. Whereas the other path consists of no items or enemies but leads to the exact same place.   Do you choose the safe path or the dangerous path with greater profit?   Unlike the previous section regarding how to psychologically control the player, this is entirely dependent on the player's personality as the value on all incentives will have a different weight to the individual.

Now, one thing I need to mention before going any further into meaningful decisions is that not all games require the existence of meaningful decisions in the first place.   For example, adding meaningful decisions to the average rhythm game could completely destroy the concept.   With a rhythm game you generally hit the displayed icon at the correct time, and using only this simple set up, the game can still be very entertaining and have a large market. Breaking it down into basic categories, rhythm games have no meaningful decisions, puzzle games and strategy games have easily viewed meaningful decisions, and action and fighting games have more quickly rotating and dynamic meaningful decisions to them.

Things to keep in mind when…

Creating situations with meaningful decisions: Is your incentive for players strong enough to make a fork in decisions and not so strong as to have no difference in the paths players choose? How much does your game actually require meaningful decisions?

6. Have Access to Any and All Knowledge

As I mentioned in the beginning of this book, a veteran Game Designer told me many years ago that the job of a Game Designer is to do everything a Programmer, Graphic Artist, Sound Designer, etc. do not do.   In my years as a Game Designer I have also found myself having no choice but to do some programming, create graphical content and even edit or create simple audio despite having no background or experience in sound design.   Not limited to those, I have also done motion capture, handled production issues and done excess amounts of localization work, including that of languages I do not actually speak. . So basically, in my experience, a Game Designer's work is *anything and everything*, and I don't think anyone can be 100% prepared for that.   Nevertheless, you can ensure that you have some knowledge of many things and more importantly *know how to further your own knowledge* of any subject.

In this day and age, internet search engines are one extremely common way of accessing knowledge.   However, relying solely on internet search engines for large topics can also be a poor choice in some situations.   If you're designing a realistic factory, go take a tour of a factory.   If you're programming a man throwing a ball, perhaps playing catch ball would give a better hint as to how catch ball should actually feel, even more than a defined mathematical equation as to how a ball should be thrown and received and affected by gravity and wind.

Put simply, knowledge and experience can be exactly what forms the actual experience each user has when playing a game.   Even if you believe your ideas are completely new and original, never before done, there are most certainly pieces and parts of your idea similar to something that has been done in the past.   And when creating these ideas or explaining details to a person, don't be afraid to reference existing games, media, historical events, people and places.

One other thing to keep in mind is as a Game Designer you must always keep learning. Simply knowing about each technological breakthrough, each large news event in any country in the world could be exactly what you need to create a better and more entertaining experience for your users.

Things to keep in mind when...

Learning something new: Is what you're trying to learn worth what amount of time it will take and will it add to your current project? Above I went into some detail about the importance of learning about anything and everything, but also make sure a large portion of that time is also being put into learning what may be of more immediate help to you.

Exercise for learning something new: Try learning one new fact or theory about a single subject each day for a full week.   At the end of the week try to explain what you've learned to another person, and put what you've found into words.

7. Think, Don't Act like a Producer

On the majority of projects in existence, producers are not developers and don't even get themselves overly involved with the developers. There are exceptions to this, but most producers aren't on a project to be creative or make something fun. Nevertheless, there are issues producers have to think about that can trump the development side of things, including even the main concept in some cases. Funding and permission are some very important matters to consider. If you are working with other companies, perhaps those licensing their products to you, the approval of many other people may be necessary for nearly every step of development. Some things they will make clear before development starts, but there are always large grey areas and sometimes completely out of the blue requests. Of course, it is impossible to predict everything that could happen outside of development, but be sure to have a rough idea of how much your plans may cost and what kind of outside problems could occur due to your ideas.

As a Game Designer you should always be aware of general costs, possibly trademarked material and other outside issues that could technically cause great problems in your projects. On top of which you should think of possible solutions to these potential problems aside from simply having a near unlimited financial resource.

But at the end of the day you need to remember you are a Game Designer, not a producer.   Your job is to make something more entertaining and fun at all costs.   But making sure you can get as much of this content into a game as possible does require that you cover your bases and know how to resolve producer issues when they do arise and when you have to clash with any producers on your projects.

Things to think about…

Exercise for producer issues: Look up 10 items you might want to use in a game that are actually trademarked.   This can include anything from household items to types of jets and tanks, etc.   Then think of all the possible solutions to resolve each of those copyright issues.   This can include changing the design or the names or finding inexpensive ways to actually use such copyrighted material.   Try to come up with a different method of resolution for each item.

8. Importance of Innovation

Some people cringe at the word innovation believing that it is simply not necessary and rehashing the exact same game with different characters is the best way to go.   If this were true then the vast majority of games since 30 years ago would consist of characters jumping on enemies to defeat them and running only from left to right.   These games certainly have their charm and there are some successful titles with very little innovation, but copying an existing game and just replacing it with different characters or graphics is not the best approach to take if you consider yourself to be a Game Designer or a creator of any kind.

Simply ask yourself the question, if you made a complete copy of your favorite game without innovation, would it be better than the currently existing game from which it was copied? Chances are a game that came out years later which is for all intents and purposes no different, would not be overly welcomed to most people aside from avid fans on the initial game, and even in that case would not please them more than the initial game itself.

That said, any project should include some gameplay mechanic or gimmick or design that really sets it apart from existing games.   This doesn't necessarily mean that innovation has to come out of thin air; in fact, it could simply be putting together two existing game features in order to create something new and innovational.

One thing people who believe they are innovational claim is that they only want to make new games, and do not want to work on anyone else's projects or existing titles.   This, much like people who don't want to make new games and only want to work on existing projects is counterproductive to becoming a great Game Designer.   If you had a chance to work on a sequel to your favorite game or a chance to make your own brand new game, this should be a predicament.   Innovating something old to please existing fans and gain new ones to the point where the sequel is even better than the original is one of the most challenging and rewarding tasks for any Game Designer. However, making something brand new also gives a Game Designer a sense of freedom to bring about easier innovation for projects.   I believe someone who can work well and be innovative in either of these situations is the type of Game Designer you should aim to become.

Things to think of when being innovative...

Does your innovation match the concept?: Simply being innovative is not helpful unless it fits with the theme and idea that drives the game itself.   Make sure your ideas fit with the theme before trying to force them into the game.

Think outside the box: Innovation might come in the strangest forms and from the strangest places.   Random brainstorming can bring about some extremely innovative ideas.

Talk it out: Be sure to put your innovative

ideas into words and talk it out with someone else involved in the project.   Putting your ideas into words really makes it feel more real and helps to identify holes which need to be filled as well as points which could easily be used to expand the innovation of the idea.

Innovation exercise: Write down 10 game genres, 10 game mechanics and 10 world or character settings and then randomly draw one of each from the piles and come up with an innovational game idea from these three elements.

9. Simplify

People tend to easily fall into the misconception that complex is better than simple. This happens not only in Game Design, but in almost all fields of employment. Often people want to avoid simplification due to the common relation between the words simple and dumb; such as dumbing down a complex theory. However, if your work requires other people to understand what you have to say, then making things simple is a necessity.

Some areas which can often become unnecessarily complex in games include story-telling, overly complex programming, character designs which have parts and colors that make it hard for people to remember who looks like what, AI for enemies to target characters based on situations most users can't even conceive, and so on.

Aside from in the games themselves, you may often find yourself working with people or companies from other countries who speak other languages, and using "big words" can actually cause more harm than do good.   The same could be said for scientists who make scientific breakthroughs and cannot simplify their findings to the point where any practical use could be made from these breakthroughs.   Thus, when simplifying your work, be sure to keep explanations relatively short and stay away from unnecessary and undefined terminology as well as give examples where possible.

You will often find that when a person cannot simplify an idea or theory, that person probably does not fully understand it himself or herself.

Things to think about when simplifying…

Who is going to review your simplified data?: Are you explaining your Game Design ideas to other Game Designers, or perhaps to programmers or artists?   How and by how much you simplify your data may differ depending on with whom you intend to share the data.   If it is fixed information for the game itself, will the player understand?

Exercise for simplifying: Think about a subject which you believe yourself to be very knowledgeable about, and find someone who knows next to nothing about that subject and try to explain a more complex concept from that subject as simply as possible to that person. For example, explaining to a 70 year old computer illiterate person how IP addresses actually work.

10. Problem Solving while Keeping out the Mongoose

One of the most famous Game Designers of all time once told me that a good idea is an idea that must solve multiple problems at once.   One of the main purposes of this is that solving a problem can often bring about new problems, and without thorough research the solution can simply increase the amount of problems. Throughout history this has always been this way.   For example, in 1883, Hawaii imported 72 mongooses from Jamaica to get rid of rats damaging the sugarcane.   However, an oversight in this plan was that mongooses were active during the day and rats during the night so they barely even met-- Which as discussed earlier would also have been terrible multiplayer map design.   On top of this, these new mongooses apparently bring about tens of millions of environmental damages every year to this day.   Thus, a poorly researched solution with the intent of solving a single problem ended up not only not solving the initial problem but also causing a completely new problem.

In games this could be trying to solve a problem by adding a new feature. Adding this new feature could possibly solve the problem, but how much time does it take to implement, and what are the possible side effects it has, what if it causes a freeze or stop in the game? If your solution solves more than one problem it gives your idea all the more weight and power.

In the hopefully rare situation where a new problem does arrive due to your work, make certain that you share this immediately with other parties involved to help you solve the new issue and be sure to start with the result rather than starting with explaining step by step what happened.

What's important when problem solving…?

Identifying the problem: A problem can be any number of things and can be technical or it could be an opinion based on feeling which could be far more difficult to identify. If the problem is that a certain area of the game simply does not feel up to the set standard of fun, then try and figure out exactly why the game doesn't feel fun at that point.   Identify what makes other areas in the game fun and make it clear for yourself and anyone else involved in trying to solve the problem.   When you come up with a solution, make certain it achieves what you set out to do and more.   Perhaps your idea can make that area more fun and actually reduce slowdown and lag in the area also solving a more technical problem which had been encountered.

11.   Straightening Priorities

This is something you need to get straight as quickly as possible to avoid unnecessary agony. And reading this chapter may come off as a warning to many that the game industry is very stressful and has many problems and misconceptions.

First ask yourself "What would you sacrifice and for what kind of project?"

One of the more successful Game Designers/Directors I have worked with, had previously worked on one of the highest rated games ever from that company, followed by one of the highest selling games (over 8 million copies) from that company, and at the time was working on a game that ended up selling approximately 100 thousand copies, which to that company was not a lot.   Nevertheless, for a small event for the promotion of this game, he had to go on a trip which caused him to miss the birth of his first child.   I also know other game developers who have missed their children's births and other life events they would have liked to attend.   However, in the game industry this is not entirely uncommon.

Another major sacrifice is daily time.   One project I was on I was working 20 hour days 7 days a week for at least half a year straight.   A lot of the time a project will be extremely demanding and require you to work long hours for little or no pay, and sometimes not even be 100% legal.   However, these situations are far from uncommon in the game industry.   Many companies will tell you they don't allow such things, but I guarantee at least half of those companies have situations where you will be required to work more than 100 hours in a single week.   Even if you are self-employed and making a game all by yourself, there may be deadlines that require you work far more than you would like to have to work.

This brings us back to the acronym I mentioned near the beginning of this book: PIFA (Persistence, Intellect, Flexibility, and Acceptance).   Let's take a quick look at each of these qualities.

Persistence is perhaps the most important

feature for a Game Designer. You have to keep trying and trying until something gets done and gets done with at least a certain level of quality. Sometimes this means doing the same thing over and over again until it finally works out; which is how many people will define insanity. Persistence to the point of insanity.

Intellect includes existing knowledge, the potential for gaining new knowledge and the innovation required to overcome the vast amount of problems that you must solve in order to effectively do your job.

Flexibility includes pretty much everything you can imagine, especially ability and schedule. Aside from much of what was mentioned above with major time constraints, ability is also constrained or tested in various ways. Perhaps you are an expert with a certain software but that is for one reason or another not available at your current place of work. However, you are still expected to be able to get something done within the week. This means you may need to give up a lot of time, learn a brand new software very quickly, or maybe just intellectually come up with a different way to solve the problem at hand.

Acceptance means coming to terms in the end with what can be done and what can't be done, as well as accepting the people with whom you work.   Even if you are doing a project by yourself, you will come to a point where interaction with another human being is necessary to complete and/or sell your creation. You may find yourself working with some of the greatest minds in the industry one day and working with complete garbage another day. But if the project is important enough to you, then whether you're working with the best of the best or the worst of the worst you will need to accept your situation and find a way to complete that project.   Another matter of acceptance is realizing that the majority of Game Designers don't make nearly as much money as some media would have you believe, and that most of the best Game Designers never become famous or become appreciated, and that the average person probably will never realize how difficult your job is and will probably assume that you just sit around playing games all day.

So is the project worth it?   If every day is hell on a project, and family and friends, or time and money are more important than the project you're working on—you might want to consider changing projects or companies or even careers. It's something you will be forced to think about on each project you join, but is far easier to decide if you have your personal priorities decided beforehand.

If you have experienced many of the above agonies and still have the persistence to continue as a Game Designer, you probably are or are on the path to becoming a great Game Designer.

Something to help think about prioritizing…

Motivation: There will often be people trying to drag you down and hurt you or in some cases even destroy your career.   This is aside from the regular obstacles in life that make it hard simply being alive.   But remember, no matter what obstacles arise, you can rise above them and better yourself and those who believe in you as well as the projects in which you believe.

Exercise for prioritizing: Write down a list of what is important to you in life and try to order it numerically.   Then decide how many of those things you would be able to sacrifice and for what.   Would you sacrifice them for being able to work on a personal mobile title?   Would you sacrifice them for working on the newest game in your favorite top selling franchise?

12.   The Con-man and the Saint

There are many Game Designers who either cannot or for whatever other reasons do not do programming, create 3D models, do animations or any other aspects of actual asset creation in games, and will therefore rely solely on others to make their ideas come to life.

To you, your ideas and planning may be great, and therefore your next task is to get the assets created so you can put or have your idea put together.   However, in many situations the people you need to help you complete your work are also busy with several other tasks, or perhaps just not motivated enough with the idea you've presented.   But if you're certain your idea is interesting, solves problems and meets all the criteria necessary to fit in the game, you need to find a way to motivate other people to want to participate in your idea.

To do this you need to learn how to be both a con-man and a saint.   This means tricking people into wanting to do work for you using methods that actually make people feel better about themselves and their work.   This often means that you need to give other people credit for your ideas, or give other people other incentives for work.   For example, if your idea was to have a pendulum gimmick the player can hang onto and swing across in level filled with clocks, you might not want to outright suggest this.   But rather, try and lead the people who need to do a lot of the work of implementing this into the game into coming up with those ideas by talking about old clocks and how they look until someone else mentions the possibility of using pendulums for mobility.   Be it modelers or programmers or whomever.   It's a lot easier for people to be motivated by their own ideas than be forced into doing something by someone else.

You may often see some people in the game industry doing interviews who often say "I came up with this and that...", but these are usually the people who don't actually inspire others on their team and are more likely taking credit of other people than giving people motivation.   And motivation is an extremely powerful tool that you must share properly with others involved in the creation of a project if you truly wish for that project to succeed.   Instead of trying to take credit from others who have worked hard, try to give credit to others in order to motivate them to work hard.

Motivational speakers often use very vague statements in order to inspire a large number of people all at once.   A motivational speaker doesn't necessarily have to talk directly to one person if he or she uses an example like an elephant chained as a baby and growing up never knowing how easy it would be to break those chains.   Something like this has a different meaning to each person who hears it, but is overall inspiring.   Motivation speakers may do this simply with personal gain in mind, or perhaps they truly and purely want to help others. But sometimes people will outsmart themselves by getting caught up in the realization that they are being tricked rather than seeing the bigger picture.   If no one is actually getting hurt and the end result is preferable to all parties, then it really doesn't matter if you're being *tricked into being motivated* or not, because being motivated is a great thing.   So always look for motivation and new ways give other people motivation.

Sometimes it's a lot easier to motivate people than you may think.   Even a simple conversation with someone may be all the motivation necessary for that person to make your idea come to life with extreme precision and quality.

Some Game Designers who have mastered motivational tactics may appear as if they have done no work at all.   If a Game Designer's work is completed without anyone realizing that person has done any work at all, there is a high possibility that he or she has actually done the job extremely well.

How to think about motivation…

Know the person you wish to motivate: Make certain your method is something with a high possibility of actually obtaining results.   To do this you must know the person you're trying to motivate, at least to some extent.   Knowing a person's hobbies may make it easier.

Motivating someone who likes cars doesn't necessarily mean you need to purchase that person a brand new car, but perhaps simply talking about automobiles or races or car-related topics with that person will motivate that person to help create your work.

Make sure your priorities don't get in the way: If you care more about getting credit for your work than actually getting the work done, perhaps some of these methods are not for you. However, you should also reevaluate your priorities to make sure you know what is most important.   If your credit is more important than the project, then perhaps the project isn't up to the standards you've set for yourself.

13. Speed up with DPO (Documentation, Presentation and Organization)

Whether you're a Game Designer who focuses mostly on system, levels, UI or anything else, a lot of your time is going to be spent making documentation for things you plan to make or have already made.   Documents are used for many purposes, such as portraying ideas to get them implemented in the game, crosschecking with other documentation and data, keeping records for testing and balancing as well as for so many other situations.   It's best to have the data easily accessible so no one is troubled later when a guidebook has to be made and the developers are required to search through the game and in some cases even do black box tests to try and figure out every single piece of undocumented data.

Also, make sure you know who will see the document.   If it is for people inside the company, don't be afraid to use images you may have found from an internet search, or reference images from other games and media that would likely be copyrighted.   On the other hand, if your document is going to be viewed by the general public you will want to have more specific and detailed professionally made images.

If you are doing a presentation with your document be sure to write in big font on presentation documents, use quick and easy to understand concept images and keep your explanations simple.   And if you're doing the presentation don't try to read the portrayed document since usually the people who see the document will be able to read it in their minds faster than you can say it, which will simply end up boring them.   Presentation requires a certain level of entertainment to it, and if you are trying to entertain someone when speaking about business models you will find you'll have an extremely rough time with long drawn out boring explanations.

Another thing to keep in mind for documentation and presentation is being able to do an elevator pitch for any idea.   If you can't describe a concept in the time of an elevator ride or a short commercial (approximately 15 seconds), there is a great chance that a large portion of the information will not stick in that person's mind.   If it's in writing try to keep it under 3 lines, as you're basically asking that person to invest his or her time and or money into something.   If that something cannot catch someone's interest in 15 seconds or 3 lines, you need to rethink your opening.

To catch the interest of a person, you don't necessarily need a catch phrase, but you should have something both strong and simple enough to stand out so that it is easy for anyone involved in the project to be able to remember and even quote.   This rule of documentation and presentation is very similar to a concept.   If your main idea or mission statement is long and so full of difficult wording that you have trouble remembering it yourself, you'll find it even more difficult to ask others to keep such a thing in mind.

Organization is the third key factor in staying on track and speeding up your work and the project as a whole.   Depending on the company, Game Designers are often known as Planners, so without a doubt planning is important.   Be sure you know what you're going to do each day before the day begins. On a couple projects I've been a part of, all of the Game Designers would gather at the beginning of each morning to share what work got done yesterday and current plans for the day. Some days it seemed like a waste when sometimes people would say for an entire week "I worked on balancing the AI, and I'm going to continue that work today." However, if you are specific in what you intend to do on a daily basis, you will find it is very helpful to getting started working. So, if you can, talk it out with anyone working with you it will help get you on track. There will probably be many situations where you might not always make it because of external problems, but getting yourself on track and on schedule is important for each morning. Sometimes you may find you get more done than you ever thought you could, which gives you more time to dabble in new and creative work.

Just like with a concept and target audience, be sure your goals are specific and measurable so you know when you can meet them and when you have met them. Game Designers have a lot of impact on the balance and overall fun of each element in the game, and these things are usually quality over quantity, thus making them extremely hard to be specific about when measuring.   However, something like finding another person, preferably another Game Designer to review your work and give an honest opinion regularly would be immensely helpful.

When considering DPO remember to...

Take on documentation when you have spare time: If someone on the team is in charge of the player characters or enemies and doesn't have documentation for them, see if you can take the time to create that documentation in place of that person.   Ask how you can find the numbers or data for the player, and create a document that can be shared with the team to not only speed up your own future work but also the work of others on the project.

Presentations require practice: If you are a bad public speaker but are still forced to do a presentation in front of a ton of other people try to practice beforehand.   There are some situations where you will have a bad boss who will give you no information about the presentation until the actual presentation begins, but even then you can get yourself into a mood for public speaking to make things easier when trying to work through your own ad lib.

Try to stay ahead of schedule: Creating a schedule is great and helpful for being organized and staying on track, but as a Game Designer you may often be handed random new jobs, especially if you are known to the company as someone with a wide range of skill sets.   If your schedule is so packed and you're already falling behind and handed new work that you cannot turn down you may end up being criticized for falling behind later.   In this case you should be sure you find a way to keep your schedule from getting overly packed, or be certain to stay ahead of your own schedule.   If you are nearly a day ahead of your own schedule each week you should be able to take on any curveballs easily.

Review your goals: Even if you can't talk over your progress and goals with others, be sure to review your own progress each morning and have already decided what you intend to do that day.

Exercise for DPO: Try creating a handwritten task checklist for a day's work or a week's work. Check off each task as it gets completed.   This could even be for tedious chores at home, such as doing the laundry or cleaning the toilet.

14.   Understanding the Gravity of Tools

In more recent years of Game Design there are countless tools you may be using when creating a game.   Most companies or even personal projects these days will use various tools and Game Engines for creating assets and data.   Sometimes these tools and engines will be in-house only and you won't be able to practice or use them outside of your place of work.   However, having used various engines and tools professionally, I can safely say that although the controls and processing may be different, the majority of Game Engines or widely used tools will all have the same basic purpose and thus being proficient in one or two will help you with almost any future instances of using tools.

Although these days Game Engines handle a lot of processes for the user, there is a saying that comes to mind, "a tool is only as good as the user."   Thinking about this statement from various angles also causes one to consider what could be done without the tool in use.   Of course tools make things a lot easier and faster and trying to reinvent the wheel is rather absurd, one should also be aware of just how much the tool does for a person.

One of my first game creating experiences was back when I was a student and I was trying to make a simple 2D side scrolling game using only text from programming without any Engine assistance.   The first time I implemented a jump function in the game was something that really caused me to think about game development more deeply.   I programmed in a jump function, and tested it out for the first time only to have a somewhat surreal experience.   The circle character jumped into the air and simply stayed there, not coming back down.   This was the first time I realized that gravity doesn't exist unless I make it exist.   And even if it does exist, how it exists is up to me.   It doesn't have to be $9.81 m/s^2$, or even a constant.   The realization of this power and responsibility is something that Game Designers who have only ever developed with tools which handle the basics may never get the chance to experience.   But I think this sense of responsibility and necessity to look at each aspect from all possible angles when creating parts of what could be considered a new world is something every Game Designer should take the time to consider.

Some recommendations for tools…

Game Engines: Most of the more well-known Game Engines such as Unreal or Unity will have features you will find in almost all Game Engines. Using the latest version of either of these engines will be useful and great experience for those still learning or not yet using Game Engines.   In my experience, if either of these engines are actually being used, usually Unreal is used on larger projects and Unity for smaller projects.

3D Modeling: Professionally you will find that products like Maya and 3DS Max are some of the most common.   Even companies that have been using other 3D software have recently been making the move to Maya.   Most of the companies I have worked for or with have used Maya more than 3DS Max, so if you had to choose one I would recommend Maya.

Documentation: This may come as a surprise to people not in the game industry, but many of the largest companies commonly use products you may already have, even if you have never even considered getting into Game Design, such as PowerPoint and Excel for documentation, or Word for story writing.

15.   Remember to Have Fun

   A lot of the philosophies for a great Game
Designer up until this point have been rather
serious and strict.   However, you are creating
something fun for people, to be entertainment
and bring people joyful experiences in life,
perhaps even something some people can look
back on years later as a great memory.   But
how can you expect to bring people joy and fun if
you cannot have fun yourself.

   When creating a game you should be able to
smile and laugh every day. Smile when
something goes well, laugh when it doesn't.   If
an AI controlled NPC character keeps running
into walls or jumping off cliffs while making a T-
pose in the middle of the game's most serious
scenes you should most definitely laugh out loud.
Maybe even show other people around you.   Of
course, you'll probably want to fix those things
as soon as possible, but even though it's more
work you have to do and more time you'll have
to put into your project, maybe it was worth it for
that laugh and memory for yourself.   Being able

to see something in the game that hopefully people outside the company never would.

Aside from enjoying things that just happen to occur during the game, perhaps try putting in spontaneous gimmicks into a level or erratic behavior into an enemy AI, or simply placing items in the game in funny places.   Of course if it's anything that could be potentially controversial you should make sure to either check with the team or take it out later.   But creating enjoyable little fun factors when you have the time is something that can keep a person creating fun and great content, and sometimes the spontaneous ideas actually turn out to be something amazingly fun and kept in the final game.

It probably sounds extremely easy to just enjoy the little things.   But this may in fact be one of the hardest philosophies to follow.   Many Game Designers who sacrifice so much and pour themselves into projects with little return will easily fall into severe mental illnesses and/or find themselves battling with physical health and bodily diseases brought on by stress.   In theory, being able to enjoy the little things and smile and laugh each day should at least keep a person slightly healthier while working.

So remember…

Always make the time to have fun when making someone else's fun.

Every time anyone ever disagrees with you from now on, you are wrong…

The meaning of this is simply to always consider the vast amount of possible points of view in existence. Even if you know for certain you are indeed 100% right, if someone disagrees with you, there is generally to be a reason. You have to consider why someone may believe that wrong is right. It could be an unlimited number of reasons, but understanding why someone may think this way is important. When creating games there will always be people who disagree with certain choices, and when the game is released there could be millions of people who disagree with certain choices.

The effort to understand is the key to growth, because the moment you assume you are correct is the moment you stop thinking, you throw away your chance for growth.

www.ingramcontent.com/pod-product-compliance
Lightning Source LLC
Chambersburg PA
CBHW070609290526
45790CB00002B/837